RAINY DAY PROJECTS

Contents

Making Paper

Paper is made from recycled fibrous material, this could be newspaper, computer paper, sugar paper, mashed up pot pourri or leaves. You will need a small picture frame and an adult with a staple gun to help you make a paper making tray. The size of the picture frame will be the size of the sheet of paper you make, so bear that in mind when you choose your frame. Once you have mastered the art of paper making you can experiment with colours and textures. Try laying pressed flowers on the wet sheet of formed paper or using different coloured material. Food colouring can be used to colour paper to good effect.

You will need:

Staple gun

Fabric

Wooden picture frame

Torn up pieces of
sugar paper

Kitchen blender

Container

Newspaper

Kitchen cloths

Rolling pin

1 To make a paper making frame ask an adult to staple a piece of fabric taut over the back of a wooden picture frame.

2 Tear the paper up into small pieces and place it in the blender. Cover well with water. Blend until the paper is well mashed. Ask an adult for help with the electric blender.

3 Pour the well watered down paper pulp into a container large enough to take the paper making frame. You will need enough pulp to half fill the container.

4 Lower the frame into the pulpy water and swish it around getting a layer of paper pulp into the frame. You may need to do this a few times to get the pulp evenly spread across the frame.

5 Lift the frame out of the water. Cover the work surface with old newspaper and lay a kitchen cloth on top of it.

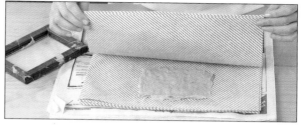

6 In one movement tip the pulp out of the frame. You may need to give the frame a knock to get the pulp out. Place another kitchen cloth on top of the paper and press it down firmly.

7 Press evenly and firmly down on the kitchen cloth using a rolling pin. This will remove the excess water. You have now made a sheet of paper.

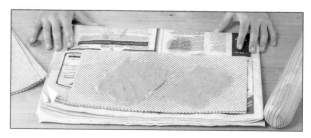

8 In this picture there are two sheets of hand made paper. You will need to practise to get the amounts of pulp right and learn how to spread the pulp evenly across the frame.

Making Ink

People have been making ink since they could draw and write. Some of the oldest books in existence were written with ink made with oak-galls - try making some for yourself. Oak-galls are the swellings caused by gall wasp larvae burrowing into leaf buds. They are found on oak trees in autumn. Give them a good shake to ensure the insects have hatched and left home. You can also use coloured fruit juice as ink – blackcurrants, raspberries and mulberries all stain in shades of red, while daffodil petals make a yellow ink. If you wanted to be secretive, try writing a letter in lemon juice. Once the writing has dried, you can bring up the message by ironing the paper with a warm iron. The message will colour brown and you will be able to read it.

You will need:

Oak-galls, soft fruit or petals

Pestle and mortar

Jar

Water

Rusty nail

Piece of muslin

Lemon

Paper and pen

1 You will need to find some oak-galls to make this ink. Pick them in the autumn after the insects have flown. Two or three oak-galls will make a couple of tablespoons of ink. Put the oak-galls in a mortar and crush them using a pestle.

3 You can use dark coloured fruit juice as ink. Use a dipping pen to write with. Blackcurrants, raspberries and mulberries will give shades of red and you can make a yellow from daffodil petals. Try different vegetables – beetroot gives a good colour.

2 Place the crushed oak-galls in a jar and add a tablespoon of water for each one and one rusty nail. Leave the mixture to stand, uncovered. After an hour you will notice that the liquid begins to change colour. By the next day it should be quite dark and in a week it should be nearly black. Strain the ink through a piece of muslin and it is ready to use.

4 To make invisible ink you can use lemon juice. Squeeze the juice of half a lemon into a small container. Use a dipping pen or a thin paint-brush. Write your message on a sheet of paper and leave it to dry. To make the writing visible you will need to iron it, the writing will turn a brown colour with the heat from the iron. Ask an adult for help with the iron.

Bottle Gardens

Create a miniature oasis in a bottle. All you need to start a bottle garden is a large, empty sweet jar and some potting compost. Choose plants which will stay quite small; ask for assistance at your local garden centre or florist. Some garden centres have bottle garden departments where they sell small plants suitable for this enclosed, small environment. Bottle gardens should never have the sun shining directly onto them (they would get too hot), but they do need to be in a light situation. Keep the soil moist. You may not need to water often if the lid is kept firmly on. Feed your bottle garden every two weeks during the summer. Decorate it using glass paints and outliners. Choose a gold outliner for a stylish pattern or use black outliner and coloured paint to create a stained glass effect on the exterior of the bottle.

You will need:

Sticks

Old spoon

Wire

Kitchen sponge

Cotton wool

A large empty sweet jar

Pebbles or gravel

Suitable potting compost

Suitable plants

Glass paints outliner

Glass paint

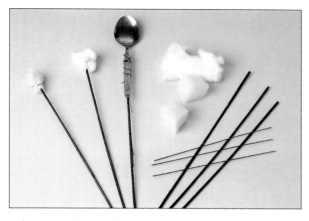

1 Begin by making some suitable bottle garden tools. For a digging tool, use an old spoon attached with wire to a long stick. Use a piece of kitchen sponge wired onto a stick to press the earth down when you are planting. Lastly, you will need a cleaning tool. For this use a piece of cotton wool wired onto a stick (you may need a few of these to tidy up the bottle garden once it is planted).

2 Place a thin layer of pebbles or gravel in the base of the bottle. This will provide drainage for the bottle garden plants.

3 Cover the pebbles with a thick layer of potting compost. Press the compost down gently using your sponge tool.

4 Use the digging tool to place individual plants in position. Press the compost down firmly around the plants, taking care not to damage their roots.

5 Use the cotton wool tool to clean up the sides of the bottle garden. Wipe away any smears or pieces of compost that have stuck to the sides of the jar.

6 Your bottle garden is now ready to decorate. Choose a simple pattern and mark it out with the outliner. The stained glass effect will resemble a mini-conservatory.

When choosing plants for your bottle garden choose low growing varieties. Keep the compost moist but do not overwater. Feed your bottle garden every two weeks in the growing season.

ICE CREAM
Sundaes

Have an ice cream sundae party for your friends. You will need a selection of ice creams, fresh fruit, custard, cream, jellies and decorative sprinkles. Try the home-made strawberry ice cream recipe, it is quick and easy to make. Fruit yoghurts can also be frozen and make tasty ice cream.

Always have an adult present when using sparklers or other fireworks.

Banana and chocolate ice cream sundae
Put one layer at a time into the glass. Start with some sliced banana, then add a spoonful of cold custard. Sprinkle on some chocolate flakes, then a small scoop of vanilla ice cream and decorate with heaps of whipped cream.

Strawberry trifle
Begin with a layer of crushed trifle biscuits. Mix 2 teaspoons of strawberry jam with 2 teaspoons of warm water and pour over the biscuits. Follow with custard then some chopped strawberries and jelly.
Finally decorate with whipped cream and a whole strawberry.

Sparkling ice cream sundae
Place a small tin of evaporated milk in the fridge for 2 hours. Pour the milk into a bowl and use a whisk to whip it until it is light and fluffy. Mix in the strawberries and syrup. Pour the mixture into a freezer-proof dish and freeze until solid. Serve it with a dazzling sparkler.

Fridge Magnets

Liven up the fridge with a bright blue teapot or a friendly teddy bear fridge magnet. These fridge magnets are made from oven bake clay, which comes in a wide range of colours.

Fruit and vegetable magnets look good in the kitchen, and a bright red apple containing a friendly little worm, will bring a smile to everyone's face when at the fridge door.

Follow the manufacturer's directions when baking the clay.

Always have an adult present when using the cooker.

1 Before you begin, make sure your hands are spotlessly clean as dirt transfers to the clay very quickly and can't be removed. Knead the clay in your hand until it is soft enough to use. Shape the teapot following the steps in the picture.

2 The bear is made from dark brown clay. Make his arms and legs from short sausage shapes. Give him a bright red nose, a bow tie or even a coloured hat! If the magnet doesn't stick, glue it on once your model is out of the oven and cooled down.

You will need:

Oven bake clay in a variety of colours

Knife

Clean surface on which to roll your clay

Small rolling pin or a suitable pen lid

Baking tray covered with foil

Magnets

Glue

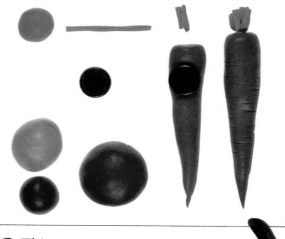

3 This carrot magnet is made from yellow and red clay mixed to give a good orange carroty colour. Make the stalk from short rolls of green clay, squashed together.

Biscuits

For a special treat, home-made biscuits decorated with icing, silver balls cherries and sprinkles, will brighten up your tea time. Try both recipes (plain and chocolate), cut out in a variety of shapes with a mixture of patterns and designs, to create a colourful plateful of delicious biscuits. A few home-made biscuits in a decorative box or bag makes an ideal gift for parents or neighbours.

1 Use a wooden spoon to mix the flour, margarine (or butter), vanilla essence, sugar and baking powder until it looks like breadcrumbs. Add the egg and mix with a wooden spoon until it forms a dough.

2 Sprinkle a little flour onto the work surface and roll out the dough with a rolling pin. Do not press too hard. Dip the cutters in flour before cutting out a selection of shapes.

3 Place the biscuits on a greased baking tray. Bake for 15 minutes at 180°C, 350°F, gas mark 4. Allow to cool and decorate with icing, silver balls, cherries and sprinkles.

Ingredients

250g plain flour

125g margarine or butter

75g castor sugar

1 teaspoon baking powder

1 egg

For plain biscuits add:

1 teaspoon vanilla essence

For chocolate biscuits add:

25g cocoa powder

You will need:

Wooden spoon

Bowl

Biscuit cutters

Biscuit decorations

Ask an adult to help when using the cooker.

Mirror Painting

irror, mirror on the wall who is the fairest of us all? Paint one of these pretty designs on a mirror tile to put up on the bathroom wall. The tiles are painted with glass paint which is available in a wide selection of colours and is very easy to use. The outliner divides the colours and comes in tubes that you use like a ball point pen, squeezing the colour gently onto the mirror.

You will need:

Mirror tiles or handbag mirrors

Glass paint outliners

Paper towel to mop up spills

Paint-brushes

Water-soluble glass paints

1 Use the outliner as if it were a pen, squeezing gently to allow a steady stream of the thick liquid onto the glass. Keep your paper towels handy in case of spills.

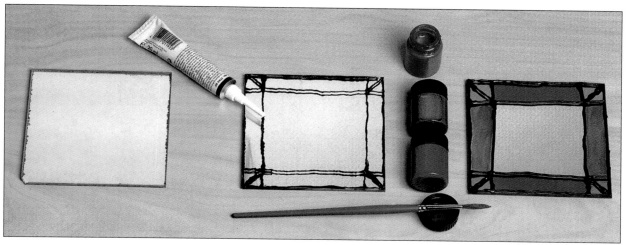

2 When the outliner is completely hard you can paint in the colour. Use a dry brush to dip into one colour at a time and wash and dry the brush well between colours.

Miniature Farm

This miniature farm can be made in an afternoon and could provide endless pleasure for a younger brother or sister. Stand it on a sunny windowsill to create a pretty country scene. Make a storage box for the farm from a matchbox covered with coloured paper and decorated in farmyard-style.

You will need:

Oven bake clay

Modelling tool and cocktail stick

Oven Tray

Match box

Coloured paper

Scissors

1 Begin by softening the white clay. Make the body first, then flatten a strip and fold it over the body as the ears. Now soften a small piece of black clay, and roll it into a sausage shape. Use the modelling tool to cut the legs and face.

2 These colourful hens are made from a small ball of brown clay. Press the clay to shape the head and tail of the hen. Make a base from a ball of green clay. Pinch out tiny pieces of red and yellow clay for the beak and comb.

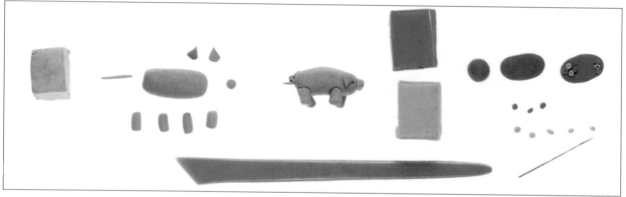

3 First soften the pink clay. Make a nice round sausage shape for the body. The pig's snout is made from a small flattened ball and its ears are made from flattened teardrop shapes. Roll out a smaller sausage shape and use the modelling tool to cut short legs. Roll out a thin tail and attach it firmly to the body.

To make some little patches of daisy-covered grass flatten an oval shape of green clay. Then make some small balls of yellow and green clay and use a cocktail stick or the tip of your modelling tool to lift them up and press them down onto the clay grass. When all your models are made, place them on a baking tray and harden them in the oven.

Follow the manufacturer's directions when baking the clay.

If you can't buy oven bake clay, you can use plasticine.

Scrunchies

Easy to make, you can have a scrunchy for every occasion. Sew them by hand in a running stitch or ask an adult to sew them for you, using a sewing machine. Thread them with elastic and decorate them imaginatively. Make scrunchies from ribbon, lace, velvet or dress fabric. A brightly coloured towelling scrunchy would be good for the seaside or swimming pool.

You will need:

Fabric and lace

Needle and thread or a sewing machine

Medium-sized safety pin

Half-centimetre wide elastic

Scissors

Sequins and glue

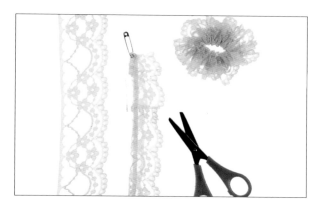

1 Lace: sew a centimetre-wide hem along one edge of the lace. Use the safety pin to thread the elastic through the seam. Tie the ends of the elastic into a knot and shape the scrunchy.

3 Tartan: this attractive scrunchy is made in the same way as the velvet scrunchy. Use matching thread to sew the seams.

2 Velvet: fold the fabric in half lengthways, with the wrong side out. Sew a seam. Turn the velvet tube the right way round by pulling one end through the other. Sew a channel in matching thread along one side and thread the elastic through.

4 Sequin: make this party time scrunchy in the same way as the tartan and velvet scrunchies. Decorate it with shiny sequins glued or sewn onto the fabric.

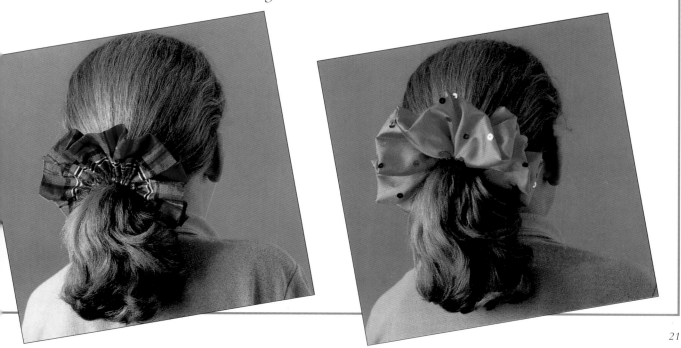

PAPER
Notepaper

Fancy writing paper makes letterwriting more fun. You can decorate paper to suit the season: make bright sunny pictures for summer holiday letters and snowy scenes for winter times. You may like to experiment with other ideas. Maybe a seaside scene or some rolling hills covered in tiny black sheep and cows would suit a holiday mood. Choose bright co-ordinated colours and matching envelopes. Use the steely glints of shiny gold or silver pens to create a night scene or even to decorate a set of paper with a firework display.

You will need:
Paper

Felt tip pens

Scissors

Glue

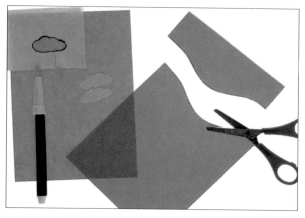

1 This summery style is made from green, blue and white sheets of paper. Decorate the sky-blue sheet of paper first. Cut out small fluffy white clouds and glue them onto the sky.

3 This snowscene is decorated with a cheerful looking snowman. Draw the snowman onto a white sheet of paper. Remember to draw the horizon onto the page.

2 Decide how low the skyline will be and draw a wavy line across the green paper. Cut away the excess paper to leave grassy green hills. Lay one piece of paper on top of the other to create the scene.

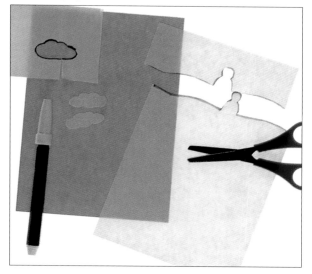

4 Use scissors to cut out the snowman and lay the sheet of white paper onto the blue sky. Decorate the snowman using a black felt tip pen, giving him a cheerful smile.

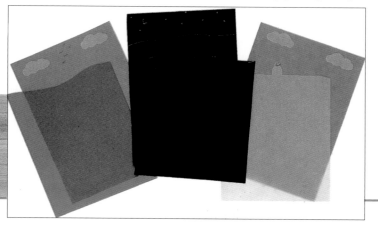

Envelopes

Y ou might have difficulty finding envelopes that are the correct size, especially if they are to match the paper and cards you have designed. Don't worry – there is no problem. Use these simple instructions and make envelopes to fit almost every size and shape of card. You could make the envelope from matching paper, patterned wrapping paper (you will need to attach a plain label for the address) or recycled paper. Decorate your home made envelopes using felt tip pens, stickers, paint or crayons. Remember to make the card first and use it to work around.

You will need:
A completed card
Paper
Scissors
Glue
Felt tip pens

1 Place the card in the centre of the paper. Fold the paper up, over the card.

2 Fold the envelope flap down, over the card.

3 Fold in the sides. Make sure the card fits the folded shape comfortably.

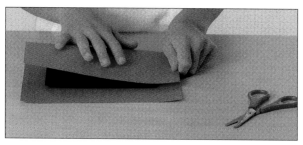

4 Cut away the excess paper from the front of the envelope.

5 Cut a flap shape.

6 Use glue to hold the envelope in shape.

Stained Glass

Create your own stained glass pictures with coloured plastic wrapping. Placed where the light shines through them these cards are most effective. Coloured wrapping film is available from craft shops, however you might want to save sweet wrappers and keep an eye out for coloured clear plastic to recycle. The holly leaves make a good Christmas card. You can have fun decorating the card with coloured glitter glue.

You will need:

Black paper

Felt tip pen

Scissors

Coloured clear wrapping

Glue and glitter glue

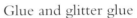

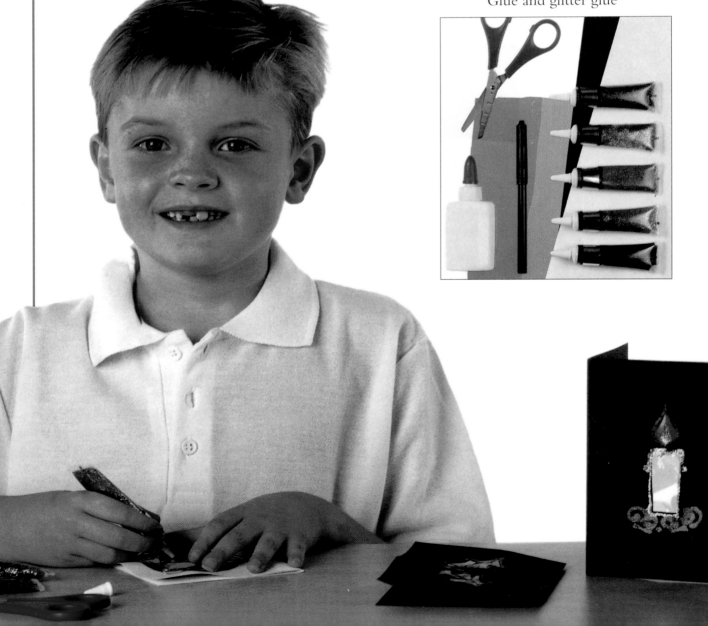

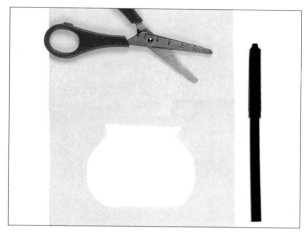

1 To make this clear blue fish bowl card begin by folding a sheet of white paper in half. Draw on a simple fish bowl shape and cut it out.

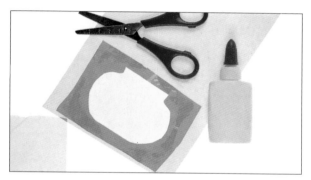

2 Cut a rectangle of blue coloured wrapping slightly larger than the fish bowl. Glue the rectangle onto the inside of the card, covering the fish bowl shape. Fold the card closed. You will decorate the cover of the card.

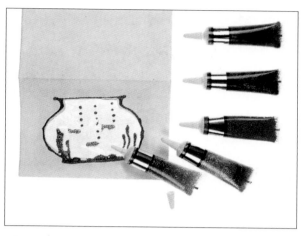

3 Use glitter glue to fill the bowl with fish, coloured seaweed and pebbles. Don't forget to paint on air bubbles. Decorate the edge of the bowl as well.

4 You will need a sheet of black paper folded in half to make the holly card. Begin by cutting out the holly leaves and berries. Cut green coloured wrapping slightly larger than the cut-out leaves and glue it to the inside of the card. Use red wrapping for the berries. Fold the card to close it and decorate the stained glass-effect card with coloured glitter glue.

If you do not have glitter glue, make your own. Use PVA glue and mix in an equal amount of fine glitter. Use a fine paint-brush to apply the glitter glue to your model or card.

Mosaic
Tablemats

Mosaics are usually created using small square tiles. To make these tablemats we have cut lots of small squares from paper and used them glued onto sugar paper to create a fishy picture. Choose bright colours to create your pictures. Squares cut from magazine pictures can also be used to make mosaics. The important thing to remember, when making a mosaic, is to keep the lines straight. This gives the impression of tiles all lined up. Use a ruler and pencil to make markings on your paper so that you can keep the squares neat and in order.

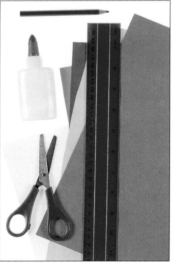

You will need:
Paper
Ruler
Pencil
Scissors
Glue

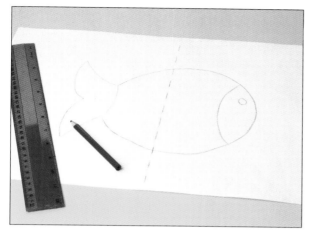

1 Begin by drawing a simple outline of a fish on your paper. Make sure that the picture is centrally placed.

2 Use the ruler and pencil to measure out squares and cut them out in your chosen colours. You will need a lot of squares.

3 Glue on the squares. Begin in a corner of the picture and try to work from one side of the picture to the other.

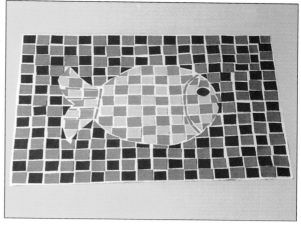

4 Your finished fish mosaic should look something like this. You could make a set of table mats for the family.

5 For a special event you might want to decorate some table napkins to match your table mats. Use paper and create pretty collage pictures.

Flowerpots

Flowerpots look good sitting along a sunny windowsill. Fill them with brightly coloured flowers to bring a little of the garden indoors. These pots are decorated with shells bought from a specialist craft shop. The shells are all recycled. The creatures that used to live in them are used as food in some countries and the shells simply thrown away. Ask at your local craft shops for them. If you gather them yourself, always check that you are allowed to on that particular beach.

You will need:

Shells

Terracotta pot or container to recycle

Grout

Spatula

Paint

Paint-brush

Glue

Varnish

1 Choose your plant pot and shells. Use a spatula to apply a layer of grout along the rim of the pot. Press the shells firmly into the grout. Leave the grout to dry. When it is dry you may want to apply a little varnish to bring out the colours of the shells.

2 These pretty pink pots have been decorated with tiny shells. Begin by painting the pot pink. You may need two coats of paint. After the paint is dry use strong glue to attach the shells. When the glue has set apply a layer of varnish to the shells.

Fishing Game

Fishing games always go down well at parties and games evenings. This fishing game is quite easy to make. The fish hooks and the fish mouths are made from paper clips. You could also make fish in two colours or make several different sea creatures, such as fish and starfish. Then players can see how many of each they can 'catch' in a given time. Another game might be to give each fish a value, adding the values at the end of the game to see which 'catch' is worth the most. This would introduce gamesmanship as each player goes for the highest value catch.

You will need:

Plate

Thick card

Thin card

Scissors

Glue

Sticky tape

Ruler

Felt tips

Sticks

String

Paper clips

1 Use a plate as an outline for a circular shape on a piece of thick card. Cut out the circle. This will be the base of the pond. Measure out a long strip of thin card for the sides. Tape it to the base.

2 The sides of the pond will prevent the fish from jumping out! Use coloured tape or felt tip pens to decorate the sides.

3 Draw the fish and starfish on a piece of thick card and decorate them using felt tip pens. Cut them out. You will need to make quite a few fish and starfish.

4 Now make the loops on the decorated stars and fish from paper clips. You will need to fold up a section of the paper clip and attach it with sticky tape to the fish and starfish.

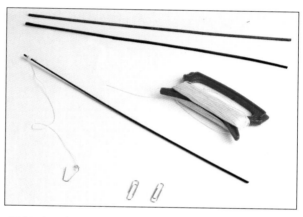

5 The fishing rods are made from garden sticks. Tie a piece of string to one end of each stick and a paper clip to the end of each piece of string. Shape the paper clip into a hook.

FABRIC AND CARD
Doll's Bed

Y ou will need a shoebox to make this comfy bed for a doll or teddy bear. The bed is made from the box and the bedhead is made from the lid. The bed will look stylish covered with brightly coloured gingham fabric or you could decorate some plain fabric using fabric felt tip pens. Cover the fabric with small flowers or draw out a patchwork spread pattern.

You will need:

A shoebox

Fabric

Scissors

Glue

Lace

Fabric painting pens

Polyester wadding

Needle and thread

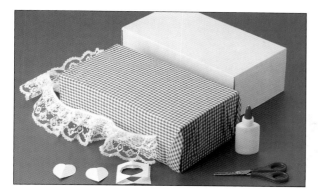

1 Turn the box upside down and cover it neatly with fabric. When attaching fabric it is a good idea to put the glue on the box rather than the fabric. Use a length of gathered lace to create a frill.

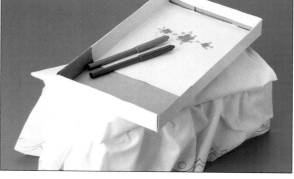

4 Gather the fabric into a frill and glue it onto the bed. Make a mattress from polyester wadding and sew on a fabric cover. Decorate the inside of the box lid to make a matching bedhead.

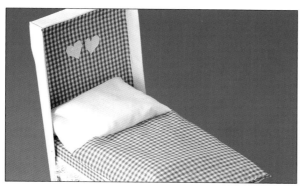

2 Stick a piece of matching fabric onto the inside of the lid of the shoebox to make the bedhead and glue the bedhead onto the base. Cut pieces of polyester wadding to size and sew on fabric covers to make the mattress, pillow and duvet.

5 To make the pillow cut a piece of polyester wadding to a suitable size, fold a piece of fabric over the pillow shape and cut out the cover. Decorate the pillow cover using fabric pens. Use your needle and thread to sew the pillow up.

3 The fabric to make this bed is decorated with fabric painting pens. Measure how much fabric you will need to make the frill around the bed. Decorate the frill with a scalloped pattern.

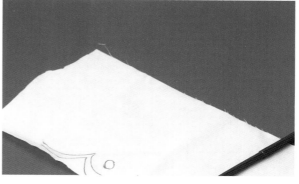

6 Make a duvet from a piece of polyester wadding and fabric. Use fabric pens to decorate the duvet cover so it looks like a patchwork quilt. Copy your scalloped design for the border.

Cloth Doll

A soft cloth doll is nice to cuddle up to and looks pretty lying on a pillow as decoration. These dolls are made from cotton fabric and are cut out in a 'gingerbread man' shape. Their hair is made from wool and they are dressed in simply shaped clothes tied with ribbon. A cloth doll can be made large, as a bed decoration or tiny, to live in a doll's house or be a 'pocket' doll. Practise painting faces on a piece of paper to get the shapes right before you paint your doll's face on.

You will need:

Fabric in a flesh colour for the doll

Felt tip pen

Scissors

Needle and thread

Polyester stuffing

Paint

Paint-brush

Wool

Ribbon

Patterned fabric for the doll's dress

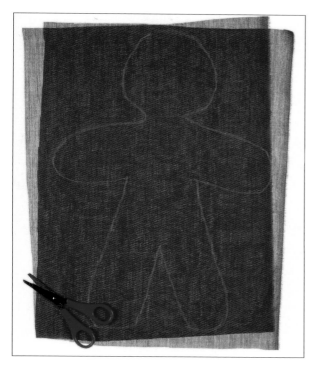

1 Draw a doll shape onto a double layer of fabric. Remember you will need a neck shape that you can sew around and cut out. Look carefully at the picture to get an idea of the shape you need to draw.

2 Sew around the drawn line, remembering to leave a gap to turn the fabric out. Fill it with stuffing, then cut the doll shape out.

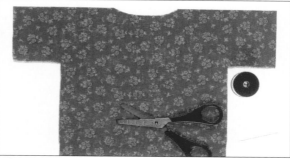

3 Use the cut-out doll as a pattern to cut a simple dress shape and sew the edges.

4 Turn the dress the right way out and sew a hem along the bottom of the fabric.

5 Dress your doll and paint on a face. Make hair by winding the wool around a piece of card then sewing a 'parting' across the middle. Attach the hair with glue.

6 Tie a ribbon belt in a bow around the waist. Now your doll is ready to enjoy.

CARD AND CRÊPE PAPER
Party Hats

Making party hats is a great way of getting the party spirit going. These hats are quite easy to make from card and crêpe paper, and can be decorated with glitter and junk jewelry. Try your hand at making a complete set of party hats for a special family meal or celebration. Make Queen and King crowns for the grown-ups and fancy coronets or colourful jester's hats for all the children.

You will need:
Thin card
Scissors
Needle and thread
Crêpe paper
Glue
Glitter
Hair band for the tiara

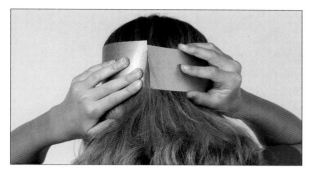

1 Cut a length of card that will go around your head with a small overlap.

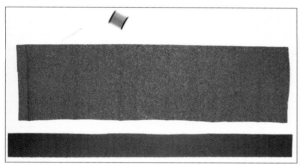

2 Next cut a wide piece of crêpe paper the length of the card. This will need to be quite wide; have a look at the illustration to get an idea of the size. Sew a line of running stitch along one of the long sides of the crêpe paper.

3 Glue the crêpe paper onto the card.

Paint pasta shapes gold or silver and decorate with glitter and use to decorate your crown.

4 Next, glue the paper-covered card into a hat shape. Pull the ends of the thread to gather the crêpe paper and tie a knot. Use crêpe paper to cover a small disc shape of card and glue that over the centre of the hat. Decorate the hat with coloured paper or card and glitter.

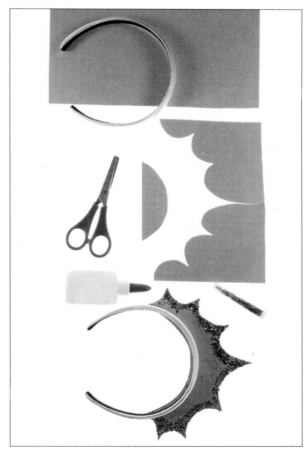

5 This sparkling tiara is made with a hair band and gold card. Lay the hair band onto the card and draw out the shape. Cut out the tiara shape and decorate it with glitter. Attach the tiara to the hair band and leave to dry.

Pencil Tubs

Use paint and glitter to decorate a useful storage tub for pens and pencils. Choose a cylinder-shaped container to recycle into a pencil tub and cover it with a layer of papier mâché to make it stronger and provide a good surface to decorate.

You will need:

Cardboard containers

Newspaper

Glue

Paint

Glitter

Paint-brushes

Scissors

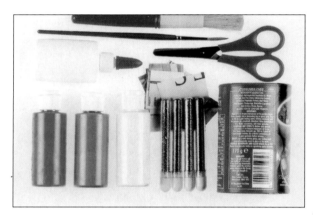

1 Start by covering the container with a layer of newspaper squares, glued on. Cover the container and leave it in a warm, airy place to dry.

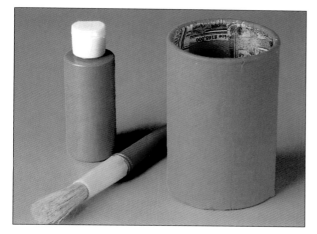

2 When the papier mâché is completely dry, paint on a base coat and allow it to dry. You may need two coats of paint.

3 Paint on the fish and seaweed, using one colour at a time. Don't forget to paint on some air bubbles above the fish.

4 When the paint is dry, spread glue on areas you want to glitter and sprinkle on the glitter. Do this one colour at a time and leave it to dry between colours.

Before you begin, give the cardboard container a quick wash. Stand it upside down to drain and then dry it with a clean tea towel.

Sewing Box

Keep needles and pins, thread and scissors safely to hand in this pretty, fabric-covered sewing box. The box is made from two layers of thick card, each covered with polyester wadding and fabric, and then glued together. When you have mastered the technique you could make a small travel sewing box to match your home sewing box. A fabric-covered box could also be used to hold handkerchiefs, hairbands and scrunchies.

1 Decide on the size of your box. Cut the base from thick card. Use the base to measure out the sides of the box and cut the lid the same size as the base. This will be the outer box. Cut out two complete sets of card. Now cut half a centimetre off around the edge of one set of card pieces. This will be the inner box.

2 Glue a piece of wadding to the four sides of the outer box and cover each one with patterned fabric. Cover the outer lid and base pieces with patterned fabric. Glue a piece of wadding to each piece of the inner box, including the lid and base, then cover these with plain fabric. (Choose co-ordinating fabrics for a stylish effect.)

3 Glue the matching outer and inner pieces together. Glue the whole box together and hold it in place with the elastic band.

4 To decorate the lid, cover a small square piece of card with plain fabric. Glue this on to the lid. Now cut a strip of fabric, cover it with glue and fold it in half lengthways, roll it up to form a grip, and glue it on to the lid.

You will need:

Thick card

Scissors

Wadding

Half a metre of patterned fabric

Fabric glue

Half a metre of plain fabric

Elastic band

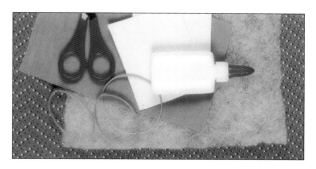

Hallowe'en

Hallowe'en is a spooky time of year. Make a hollowed-out pumpkin lantern. Carve a face on one side of the pumpkin and stand it outside your home with a lit candle inside. The golden candle light will shine through the dark! For ghoulish fun try making this very squidgy Hallowe'en game. Your friends will enjoy plenty of laughs searching the green gunge for spiders and worms. The glow-in-the-dark character worm is made from oven bake glow clay. You could make some to put in trick or treat boxes. Open them in the dark to enjoy the glow!

1 Half fill a large bowl with water. Add enough food colouring to turn the water dark green. Sprinkle 3 or 4 tablespoons of wallpaper glue onto the water. Allow the wallpaper glue to sink to the bottom and then stir gently with the spoon until the mixture is sloppy and thick.

2 Add the spiders and toads and the game is ready to play. Take turns to feel through the gunge and guess which creature you are fishing out.

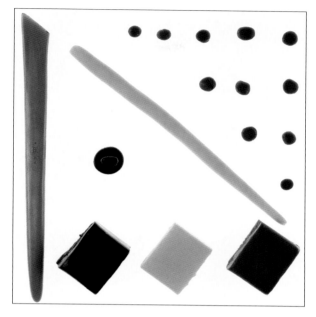

3 Make the cute little glow-in-the-dark worm with special oven bake glow clay. Make the body first, then form it into the worm shape. Make a number of small ball shapes in dark green and flatten them. Press them onto the worm. Make a hat and place it on the worm's head. Bake the completed model according to the manufacturer's instructions. You could stand the finished worm on a shelf as an ornament or turn him into a fridge magnet or brooch.

You will need:

Bowl

Water

Green food colouring

Wallpaper glue

A selection of plastic toads and spiders

Oven bake glow clay

Pumpkin

Knife

Candle

FESTIVAL CANDLESTICK
Hanukkah

Hanukkah is the Jewish festival of lights. It is celebrated as a reminder of the time 2000 years ago when the Jewish Temple was destroyed in battle by the Syrian king. When the battle was over the Jewish people repaired the Temple and went to light the oil lamp which burns in front of the Ark. They found they had hardly any oil, only enough for one day. But, by a miracle, the oil lasted eight days, long enough for the people to prepare more Holy oil to burn. Nowadays Jewish families celebrate Hanukkah in December for eight days, lighting a candle each day until they are all lit. Then they enjoy a time of celebration with parties, games and gifts. You can make a small Hanukkah candlestick to stand on a windowsill. Keep it lit through the festival.

1 Divide your clay into thirds. Roll two thirds out into a long rectangle. Cut out a zig-zag pattern to make the base of the candlestick. Flatten the edges of the zig-zag so that the candlestick will stand securely. The remaining third of the clay will make the candleholders. You will need one candleholder in the centre and four on each side of it.

2 Assemble the candlestick and leave it in a dry, warm, airy place before decorating it.

3 The candlestick is decorated with paint and glitter. Ask an adult to help each day. First light the centre candle and use that to light the other candles day by day. On the first day light one candle, on the second light two candles and so on, until the eighth when all eight candles will be lit.

You will need:

Air hardening clay

Modelling tool

Paint

Paint-brush

Glitter

Candles

Measurements

TEMPERATURE

Fahrenheit	Centigrade
250–300	120–150
300–350	150–175
350–375	175–190
375–400	190–200
400–425	200–220

LENGTH

cm	ins
2.5	1
5	2
7.6	3
10	4
12.7	5
15	6
17.7	7
20	8
22.8	9
25.4	10

WEIGHT

oz	grams
1	30
3	75
6	175
8	250

This is a Parragon Book
This edition published in 2002

Parragon
Queen Street House
4 Queen Street
Bath BA1 1HE, UK

9780752584027

Produced by Miles Kelly Publishing Ltd
This edition and cover design by Design Principals, Warminster

A copy of the British Library Cataloguing-in-Publication Data
is available from the British Library.

ISBN 0-75258-402-2

Printed in China

RAINY DAY PROJECTS

Vivienne Bolton